To the Glory of His Name!

A Book of Poetry, Prayer, and Praise

BY MARIAN COLTON

DORRANCE
PUBLISHING CO
EST. 1920
PITTSBURGH, PENNSYLVANIA 15238

Dorrance Publishing Co
585 Alpha Drive
Pittsburgh, PA 15238
Visit our website at *www.dorrancebookstore.com*

ISBN: 978-1-6386-7293-7
eISBN: 978-1-6386-7644-7

All poetry, prayer, and praise as well as photography provided by Marian Colton

To the glory of God!

Father, Spirit, Son
Blessed "Three in One";
Glory to Your name!

My life is sweetly blessed;
In You I take my rest.
Glory to Your name!

My heart I give to Thee,
oh Sacred Trinity!
Glory to Your name!

I dedicate this book to my brother Joey's memory.

I learned more about the love of God while caring for my elder brother (who was a Down Syndrome individual) during the last seven months of his life than I had in all of my own fifty-two years on this earth!

I also wish to acknowledge my parents; they modeled the unconditional love of Christ and shared His grace and mercy with complete abandon...

Our family is blessed!

All that I am and all that I do is a direct result of their influence in my life.

A special "Thank you" to my husband, my friend, and my colaborer in God's Kingdom.

Christopher P. Colton, you are truly a man after God's heart! You have always been an example for me of what a disciple's life should look like. It is an honor to serve along side of you in both the Good News Nursing Home Ministry and the Special Needs Ministry of Calvary Lighthouse Church.

Your support, unconditional love, and vast amounts of encouragement are what have carried me through the five-plus years it has taken me to see this project to fruition. With you as my life partner, I am truly blessed!

In His love and with all of mine,

Marian

"Thank You"

Thank you, Folks, for all you do.
God ministers his love through you.

You share his mercy and his grace.
His light shines brightly through your face.

Your openness to share Christ's love,
brings happiness to God above.

You've heard the Lord and obeyed the call
To share his mercy with one and all.

You share his love, speak of his Grace.
You call them in to take their place.

The Father knows; the Father sees.
His heart is full; his spirit pleased.

"Thank you, child, for all you do.
My Kingdom grows because of you."

M.C.

This poem was composed as a tribute to both the Special Needs Ministry team members and those of the Good News (Nursing Home) Ministry team.

It was read to them at the February 18th luncheon. Copies were given to team members as well as Special Needs family members.

A Poet's Prayer

March 11, 2012

Let my words, "draw them in"
to see you, Lord, and repent of sin.

Allow my thoughts to cause
a burning desire
to know you, Father, and to
Heaven aspire.

Use my hands to "pen"
your words,
and to offer the Gospel
so it will be heard.

I'll pen it in poetry,
Write it in Prose.
I'll speak of Salvation
until everyone knows!

You gave me a gift;
now I must use it.
To speak of Salvation
and my decision to choose it.

The words that I write
Come straight from my heart,
to draw others to you
and a relationship start!

Be with me, Lord,
as I write and I pray.
Open their hearts
so they hear what I say.

I offer up this gift to you.
May the things that I say
restore and renew.

May the Kingdom grow
and lives be changed,
hearts restored and "rearranged"!

I've got a Choice...

March 2012

I've got a reason
to be angry with you.
But, is that what
I want to do?

It isn't my Father's
plan for me.
He desires to see
forgiveness flow free!

What you've done
and the things you have said
disturb my heart
and are "in my head."

But forgiving you
is what's truly best.
It cleanses my soul
and keeps my spirit at rest.

So, I've made my choice
and I choose to forgive.
To love like Christ
and in His Spirit live.

"Open Your Gift."

"Jesus is Lord!"
I know this full well.
But, to share this with others
I must, "Go and tell"...

I'll write it in poetry,
Share it in prose.
I'll offer the Good News
'til everyone knows!

The Lord is my shelter.
Faith in Him is my story.
My writing is the resource
to give God all Glory!

What gifts or which talents
has God given to you?
Use them to praise Him
in all that you do!

Your gift He has given
so your praise is your own.
None other could scatter
the seeds you have sown.

Bless the Lord with your art,
with your words or your song.
Praise His name, give Him glory
all the day long!

A gift that's been given
but has never been used,
is a "slight" to the giver
and leaves their heart feeling bruised.

So, open your gift.
Use it often and well.
Glorify God and the "Good News" do tell!

June 17, 2012

This poem is dedicated to "the Ladies Who Crochet" of Calvary Light-house Church. Their use of their talents/gifts are the pebbles tossed into God's Lake of Love,

A Prayer for Discipleship

Lord, let me find happiness in doing your will.
Let me not seek it in other people.

Let my walk be your walk, and let each of my footsteps leave visions of you.

Let each of my words leave echoes of your voice.

May my smile shine with your light, and my fragrance linger with your power and strength.

Let my every endeavor be for a Holy purpose; nothing is of value that isn't done to the glory of the Most High.

May you always be glorified through my life, and may I ever remain humble.

Amen.

"Thank you, Mom and Dad"

Mom and Dad, you gave to me
a love for God
and my family.

You taught me how to love
and pray.
You shared with me
your hearts each day.

I never felt alone or "blue,"
because
of all the love from you.

As parents go,
you were the best!
Facing many trials,
without taking a rest.

Your life was hard;
but your hearts were true.
Life's challenges took
no toll on you!

God must be smiling,
of that I'm sure!
You served Him well,
with motives pure.

You raised your children
as best you could.
You loved the Lord,
just as you should.

Your children learned
so much from you!
Now the Lord is part
of all that we do!

Praise from a Thankful Heart

Praise you, Jesus, for my soul!
It was shattered; now it's whole.

Your life you gave for my sin.
Now I'm holy from deep within!

Without a doubt, You are my Savior,
Loving me to good behavior.

You loved me even when I was "low down";
But now in Heaven I'll receive my crown!

Thank You for your love so true;
My life, my trust, I give to you.

I'll praise You for eternity;
Thank you, Lord for loving me!

Lord, I live my life for you.
You're part of everything I do.

My heart, my soul, my spirit too
Are dedicated just to you!

Your life you live each day through me,
To touch the lives of all I see.

My hands and feet are yours to use,
To serve in any way You choose.

I will go to where you send,
Salvation's plan to extend.

I'll call them in; I'll share the news
That repentant hearts You do not refuse!

When we call upon Your name
Our lives are never quite the same.

No sinner need be lost to Thee;
You've paid the cost so we'd be free!

(Feb. 14, 2008)

From the Heart of a Child

I love God, and He loves me!
 We're good friends, it's plain to see…

He makes me happy when I'm sad.
 He cares for me through Mom and Dad.

I'm never alone; He's always there.
With Him my thoughts I love to share.

Mom says, "He's just a prayer away,"
So I talk to Him most every day!

God understands me; He listens well.
So all my secrets to Him I tell.

It makes me happy just to know
I have a loving Father to whom I can go…

God's love for me is here to stay.
 He'll never leave me or turn away!

I love Him back, that's for sure,
With a love that's solid, strong, and pure!

"So take my heart, so loving and true;
Lord, today I give my life to You."

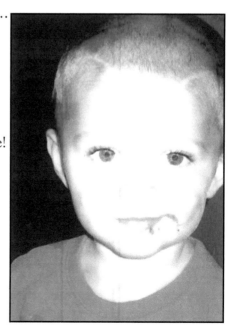

Lord,
I see them coming one by one,
From the rising to the setting sun.
They come from every walk of life,
Carrying their pain, sorrow, and strife.
They drag their feet; they move so slow,
Not really sure which way to go.

We must point the way to You;
Guide them, teach them, help them through.
We must "light the path" and clear the way;
Gather in souls to Your Kingdom, I pray.

(Feb. 2008)

I Pledge Allegiance to My Lord

I will praise you today, Lord
In thought word and deed.
I will go where you send me;
I will follow your lead.

I'll listen and obey, Lord, your every command.
When I'm tired and weary, I'll simply "just stand."
I'll stand on your promises, stand firm in my faith.
I'll stand up and praise you, or stand still and wait.

I'll lift up your name wherever I go.
Compassion and love to all, I will show.
Your hands extended forever I'll be….
Anoint me for service: true worship to Thee!

An Invitation to Enlist

They are hungry and thirsty and need a helping hand,
They are lost and lonely; they don't know where to stand.
We are to be their compass, to share with them the Way.
To lead them to His place of rest, and help them there to stay.

I'm speaking of the broken hearted, the orphan, and the blind;
 Leading these to Jesus is more than being kind…
It's giving hope to the hopeless, motion to the lame,
It's offering His mercy, forgiveness of all shame.

Jesus wants to save them, each and every one.
He'll send out His disciples until the job is done!
We'll worship; we'll disciple; we'll pray for His healing touch.
We'll testify and glorify! We love Him very much!

Won't you join our army; won't you come along?
Everyone who enters in, helps to make us strong!
Lord Jesus is our Captain; he leads us on our way,
To seek and save, restore not blame, to draw them in to stay!

Listening to the Voice of God

They walk this earth with hearts of stone,
Always feeling all alone.
They never see or hear the cry
Of hurting souls that they pass by…

God has a plan for what to do,
But we must share; both me and you!
We were meant to help and care
For everyone—everywhere!

To heal a hurt, to hold a hand
To let them know we understand.
 To create a smile, to dry a tear,
To offer strength, to allay a fear.

We are His hands; we are His feet.
We leave His fragrance; it is sweet.
He loves; He lives His life through us.
We must honor this sacred trust.

No heart of stone will I wear,
I will listen; I will care.
God will use me, I will bless
I'll give my all—nothing less!

The choice you make will set the tone
Live for God or live alone?
Alone, without God is a lonely place;
A life in Christ is filled with Grace!

No heart of stone, not deaf or blind.
Our lives we share with all mankind!
God works through us to do His deeds,
Anoints our lives for mankind's needs!

Thank you, Lord, for using me,
I'll spend my life on bended knee.
Allow me, Lord, to serve you well:
About your mercies I will tell!

A Lonely Place

I'm so alone; I know not why.
You sent your son for me to die.
I've given you my heart and life;
So why this pain? Why this strife?

My life is yours; there is no doubt.
But now I cry, I'm sad, I pout.
I know not why I feel like this.
I'm lonely and your face I miss.

Do I have some hidden sin?
Am I lacking deep within?
Help me, Lord, to find my way,
To come back home to you today.

You are waiting just for me.
Help me search; help me "see."
This feeling is so sad, so bleak.
Your joy, your hope is what I seek.

You, my Lord, are always there.
It's I who must have gone somewhere
You wait for me; I must return.
Spark a flame, and let it burn.

Show me where I went astray.
Bring me home to you today.
Tell me of your love for me.
Help me hear; let me "see."

Lord, I crave your sweet embrace.
I desire to see your face.
My strength comes from your place of joy;
Stealing that is Satan's ploy.

Fill me up to overflow
With your joy, so I shall know
A life fulfilled, a life brand new.
A life that's set to follow you.

The Holy One

You sent to us your only son,
The Lamb of God, the Holy One…
He gave his life on that broken tree,
To save my life, to rescue me…

My sins he bled and died to cleanse…
Nothing else would make amends…
My soul he saved; my life he spared,
With me, eternal life he shared.

Your only son; the Holy One
Your Only son; the Holy One

You felt such love for me alone…
For my sins did Christ atone.
Alone, he hung upon that cross
You watched him die, You felt the loss….

My life was spared, my hope restored…
Because you sacrificed, my Lord…
You've blessed me with eternal life,
Now I've become Christ's bride, his wife…

Your only son; the Holy One
Your only son, the Holy One

Jesus is the Holy One…
The risen Christ, your only son.
But I am yours; I'm family…
Because of Christ, you've welcomed me…

The love we share cannot compare....
To any love, from anywhere...
He gave his life just for me...
He shed his blood, and rescued me...

Your only son, the Holy One
Your only son, the Holy One

The Blessing That Was Joey

My brother was a special man,
For his life, God had a plan...
He couldn't speak, couldn't share,
But with his love he did declare:

"Jesus is the only way! So give to him your heart today!"

His body and his mind confused,
But mightily by God was used.
His witness to our Father's love
Drew hearts and souls to God above.

He couldn't speak, couldn't share,
But in his heart he did declare:

"Jesus is the only way! So give to him your heart today!"

The body of a man, the mind of a child,
The spirit of an angel, meek and mild.
With words he could not testify,
But eyes, and hands would glorify!

He couldn't speak, couldn't share,
But with every breath he did declare;

"Jesus is the only way! So give your heart to Him today!"

He loved the Lord with all his heart,
God's love he always did impart

To all he met: he never missed.
He was "the Silent Evangelist"!

He couldn't speak, couldn't share,
But with his life he did declare:

"Jesus is the only way! So give to him your heart today!"

Love Is a Two-Way Street

My heart is full of love for you.
You're part of everything I do.
My thoughts, my prayers, my songs, my praise.
You end my nights, begin my days!

Love is a two-way street; since Jesus and I happened to meet....

No longer am I a slave to sins.
In you, each "new life" begins.
Your bride, my Lord, I'll always be...
Both here and throughout eternity.

Love is a two-way street; since Jesus and I happened to meet....

My sins are gone; my heart brand new,
Since giving all my life to you!
Thank you, Lord, for loving me,
Throughout time and eternity.

Love is a two-way street; since Jesus and I happened to meet...

You called my name; I heard your call.
You let me know I'm your "all in all."
Your son you gave so I'd be free;
You shower your blessings and grace on me!

Love is a two-way street; since Jesus and I happened to meet.....

Marian Colton
April 20, 2007

A Hidden Song

I sat down to write a "Love Song'; but the words, they didn't come...
I searched my heart; I looked within, but all I felt was numb.
I couldn't tell what was wrong, just knew there was a hidden song...
Somewhere deep, somewhere strong, somewhere there's a hidden song...

My heart feels hard, not stone but wood,
A wise man told me this is good";
A spark can ignite and wood can burn
When to the Lord my face I turn...
Somewhere deep, somewhere strong, somewhere there's a hidden song...

Holy Spirit, It's my desire;
Ignite my heart; spark the fire.
Fan the flames of my desire,
To lift His praise stronger and higher...
Somewhere deep, somewhere strong, somewhere there's a hidden song...

Search my soul, find the song;
I shall sing it all day long....
My songs of praise shall ever be,
From deep within the heart of me...
Somewhere deep, somewhere strong, somewhere there's a hidden song...

"Passing It On..."

Speak to my heart, Lord:
I'll hear what You say.
I'll follow Your leadings;
I'll do things Your way.

My own agenda
I'll leave behind.
Your ways are better;
They're just and they're kind.

Compassion and mercy, You give to all.
No matter how burdened,
No matter how small.

You offer hope to all whom You see.
I'm grateful Your mercy,
You've poured out to me.

I'll speak of Your grace,
And share of Your love.
My focus shall be
on Your Kingdom above

Lost souls I shall gather.
Disciples I'll make.
I'll reach out to many;
There's none You won't take!

Salvation's the gift;
We must simply believe it.
It's there for the taking;
We just must receive it!

So, Lord, what You give me
Before my life's gone,
I'm sharing with others;
"I'm passing it on!"

Thoughts of Heaven...

by Marian Cotton

Herein, Lord, my passion lies...
drawing others to You.
Am I wrong to not "long"...
for Heaven?

I love You deeply,
passionately,
totally
Yet...
I do not sit
and wait for Heaven....

My passion lies
in sharing Your love with others.
Bringing them to your cross
and helping them to give their hearts to You.

Heaven is my home; I know that very well. I will enter His gates with Thanksgiving in my heart; this is true! But while I am still on this planet, I will sing His praises! I will not sit still and "wait" for my Heavenly reward. I will shine with His light and actively share His Love and Grace with those around me. "The Harvest is plentiful, but the workers are few..." If there is breath left in your body, there is a job meant for you to do. If God asks you to "do it," He will equip you for the task!

"Why I do the Things I do."

Your love for me has drawn me to you;
You are part of everything I do.
My love for You, so deep and true,
Is "Why I do the things I do"!

Your mercy and your grace abound
Form puddles deep within dry ground.
 I dip my feet and "splash around";
It sprinkles the lost with the urge to be found....

When Doubt sneaks in and creates a pall
 You lift me up; you don't let me fall...
My faith is strong, I stand bold and tall
Remembering that you died for all!

Your Spirit speaks; I must obey.
You've many plans for my life today.
You've chosen the words for me to say,
You'll bless me with them as I worship and pray!

You live your life through my hands and feet.
I must traverse many a street;
Sharing your love with all whom I meet.
Filling the empty, making those "unfinished" complete!

You love to live your life through man.
You've made us part of your Salvation Plan.
We must do all that we possibly can,
To ignite a small fire, with flames You will "fan"!

July 5th, 2008

ROBIN A. LACZYNSKI
AGE: 16 · TOMS RIVER

Robin A. Laczynski, 16, of Toms River, passed away Tuesday, Oct. 7, at Community Medical Center, Toms River. Robin was born in Neptune and had resided in Toms River all of her life. She was a student at Jackson Regional Day, Jackson.

Surviving are her biological mother, Judith Laczynski; her grandparents, Robert and Delores Laczynski; her aunt and uncle, Regina and Ronald Fernicola; her uncles, John Laczynski and Philip Laczynski; her maternal great-grandfather, Louis Lombardi; her great-aunt and uncle, Judith and Jeff Stevens; and several cousins.

Visiting hours will be from 2 to 4 p.m. today, with funeral services at 3 p.m. at the Silverton Memorial Funeral Home, 2482 Church Road, Toms River. Cremation will be private.

Robin's life has touched my own.
By knowing her, my heart has grown.

She was such a giving child,
With a disposition sweet and mild.

She loved the Lord with all of her heart;
To all she met, His love she did impart.

Her family meant the world to her.
Emotions often did within me stir
As I listened to her thoughts of love
for each of them and for God above.

Marian Colton
St. Justin's Center of Learning
This tribute was written upon the occasion of Robin's "going home"
to the Lord.

"Molded for His Purpose"

To all of God's children
Everywhere...
His love and hope
We're called to share.

To every "people group"
bring Christ's love;
and to point the way
to God above.

We're called to care,
to serve, to share.
To help Him mold them
if we dare...

We only have to hear His voice.
For when we love Him—
We've no other choice.

We are no longer
slaves to sin;
Happily so, we're bound to Him!

This was God's Word to me at the Special Touch Annual Expose' in
Waupauca, Wisconsin, on March 19th, 2009.

Where God Abides.

We look for You, Lord,
Where we'd like You to be,
Like in the shade
of a large, "leafy" tree.

We seek You in places
Where You seldom take rest.
While we're there seeking comfort,
You're off giving your best!

You're out in the desert.
You're in the midst of the storm.
We've only to look for You
Where tornadoes take form.

You're at the Beginning
And also the End.
You're a part of the whirlwind;
You "go with"; You don't "send"!

When a sandstorm strikes
And I really can't see,
I just reach out my hand;
For You're always with me.

I need not "go forth" to search for You;
You are the main part of all that I do.

"Compulsion."

The things I say,
The tasks I do;
Must always
point the way to you!

The songs I sing,
The books I read,
Must
my heart, my, soul,
my spirit feed.

I must not waste
a single day.
My life must always
point Your way!

I must guide
my friends to you;
help them, love them,
pray them through...

In the Quiet Time

Lord,
I'm reading your Word
each and every day.
I'm making the time to
worship and pray.

I'm taking a moment
to seek your face;
I'm "quieting down"
in a private place.

Please meet me, Lord;
Please spend some time.
We'll enter communion
with Joy sublime!

Your intimacy, your love
Are all that I seek,
In this world filled with chaos;
So dark and so bleak.

I've made You my haven.
Your heart is my home.
I'll stay in your presence;
No more will I roam.

You do your part, Lord.
You commune here with me.
You fill me with Hope, Lord!
My faith You set free!

I'll look to tomorrow
But live for today;
I'll stay in Your Word, Lord,
As I worship and pray.

This poem was written during the second major snowstorm of the winter 2010–2011.

The three-foot-deep blizzard of December 26th, 2010, began a weather pattern that never "let up" during the month of January. Ten-foot snow walls lined the streets, and earth/grass/asphalt hadn't been seen in over a month. The activity of shoveling had become as routine as taking out the trash.

My lips began to "grumble and complain" as I picked up my trusty shovel for perhaps the fifth or sixth time. As I looked down the street, however, my eyes beheld such a wellspring of beauty! The Lord spoke to my heart, and I chose, instead, to give thanks and praise in ALL situations! The following poem, "Snow Day," is the result.

Snow Day

In the Whiteness,
Holy Brightness,
All is still with muffled sound.
Yet, life activities are all around...

Birds flit to and from the feeder
and nibble seeds upon the snow.
Squirrels scamper up and down,
around the trees,
not sure which way to go

You can hear the distant sounds
of voices muffled (softer) by the snow.
People busied with those things of life
When there's nowhere you can go...

A shovel scrapes upon the ground,
Children's laughter all around.
My kettle whistles; I'll make my tea.
It's time, Lord, to spend some time
with Thee.

I'll "settle in" with my Bible and tea,
to read, to pray, and to worship Thee.
Lord, thank you for this day of snow.
Use it, please, to help my spirit grow.

A Mother's Garden

My son is a dad! How can that be?
Why, just "yesterday" he was a boy of three...

My sons are all grown
With kids of their own.
Please, dear Lord, bless the seeds that I've sown...

I've sown seeds of Faith, of Hope, and of Love,
I've pointed the way to Your Kingdom above.

I've lived life in service to others in need,
"Caring and Sharing" is a much-treasured seed.

Please water and nurture the values I've planted;
May my children not ever take your blessings for granted!

Let them come to the knowledge that you died for their sin;
And welcome the chance to "in their hearts take you in..."

Surround them with Christians; protect and provide.
Place Angels around them; one on each side?

I stand on your promise; my children are yours
I gave them to you with my heart years before...

Your Hedge of protection, is all that they need
'Til they harvest the blessings of their mom's spiritual seed!

This poem/prayer was composed on August 14th, 2008, the day after the birth of my grandson J.R. The event caused me to reflect upon my two sons, Michael (five-year-old grandson Jordan's dad) and Richard, the "new dad." Not to be left out, my lovely daughter Sarah, who is not yet married, is also in my prayers today!

A "Forever friend" and former coworker retired in June of 2011. I was asked to write a tribute to Trish King for her retirement celebration. As I often turn to poetry and prose, I chose to pen the following poem as my "Tribute to Trish."

This piece was one of the most difficult for me to create; I had to disentangle twenty years of memories and emotions in order to place them succinctly and fluently on one simple sheet of paper. I presented my tribute in front of sixty-plus friends/coworkers during Trish's surprise retirement party. I knew I'd captured "the moments and memories" of our times spent together as I looked around at the eyes glistening with heartfelt emotion and the smiles and nods of recognition of times gone by....

This tribute was truly an "honor" to create!

"Tribute to Trish"

Trish King is leaving;
Her teaching days done.
It's time now for spending
her "days in the sun..."

As we bid her "Farewell,"
and say a fond "Adieu,"
Let's recall what she's been
both to me and to you.

A Teacher, of course,
and a "Mentor" to many.
A Clamdigger by nature,
but so kind to this "Benny"!

When transferred to her class
I cried, "Boo hoo hoo."
Trish assured me I'd be saying,
I'd left "Anita who?"

She gave it six months
But one week's all it took.
Her caring and sharing
grabbed my heart like a hook.

The children all love her.
Adults do the same.
Reigning as "Preschool Princess"
Is her one claim to fame!

Her love for her family,
Her students and friends,
Shines bright as her tiaras.
Will wearing these now end?

As her little friend Joey has said
from the start,
"Trish King, you're the teacher
who's put a song in my heart!"

So, farewell to the Princess
Who married a King.
We wish you the best
That Retirement can bring!

Morning Song

Lord, I offer up this day to you.
Let all I say and all I do,
Bring glory, and honor, and praise
to your name,
and touch people's hearts so
they'll not be the same.

Use me, Lord, to draw others in
to a life stayed on you,
a life freed from sin.

May your symphony of love for mankind,
melodically ring through their
hearts, souls, and minds.
Have my life be an instrument
playing your song,
drawing people towards Righteousness
—turning from wrong.

August 8th, 2012

Transformation

Lord, You are near
You are here.
Why don't we see
How close You can be...?

You stick right by our side;
Yet the distance seems wide;.
We cannot hear your voice;
And we do this by choice!

Why do we hide
instead of abide?
We don't seek your face;
Choose the world in its place.

I don't understand
the focus of man;
the choices we make,
though our souls are at stake!

Lord, I'll make you my King,
surrender everything.
My heart, my soul, my life;
My sorrows, joys, and strife,

When we call on your name,
Our lives are not the same.
You enter our hearts,
and a relationship starts.

You wash away our sins;
And our "New Life" begins.
Thank you for your love,
grace, and mercy from above.

My Tribute to Toni

"Toni Bolonga" your name so endearing...
The thought of you leaving has our eyes all "a tearing"...

Always so friendly, so thoughtful and kind.
No better a para could any teacher find!

Creative, artistic, funny, and sweet,
The students who had you were in for a treat!

The first to collect for a cause or a friend,
to honor another your time and energies you'd spend.

Oh, the joys we all shared, as our children were wed!
As they gave us our grandkids, what happy tears we all shed!

As we lunched and we laughed, we've also hugged as we cried.
We've leaned on each other as loved ones have died.

Together we've seen so much of life's history change.
To think of you retiring is really quite strange.

"BUT..."
"Oh, the places you'll go—the things you will do...
Toni Martyn, our hearts and our love go with you!"

With love,
Marian Colton

A Call to "Come Home..."

My daughter, I love you
and I keep you in prayer...
But, you've left your "First Love"
and are close to despair!

Your trials are many;
Tribulations so great...
Return to your Father
Before it's too late!

God's mercy and grace
will always abound.
You walked with Him once;
Now by sin you've been bound.

Open your heart,
Let Jesus in.
He's waiting to free you,
and forgive all your sin.

You've done all those things
that you've wanted to do...
They haven't succeeded;
You're still sad and so "blue."

Return to the Father
in the name of His Son.
Let the Holy Spirit fill you
'til your revival is done!

The peace you will find
is beyond understanding;
with power to withstand
all that sin's been demanding.

The victory is yours;
It was won on the cross.
Christ Jesus achieved it,
so you wouldn't be lost!

Feb. 8th, 2012

"My Love Song to Jesus"

You, Lord are the Lover of my soul.
Alone, I was broken.
In you, I'm made whole.

Master, Creator, Lord of all things;
You were born to be Savior,
Now reign "King of Kings"!

I've given my faith
and trust unto you.
You are the main part
of all that I do.

My life I've placed
within your hand.
On each of your promises
I faithfully stand.

You are my Beginning
and also my End;
my Lover, my Brother,
my Savior, my Friend!

Feb. 3, 2012

To My Prayer Partner
With a Grateful Heart.

You prayed a simple prayer with me.
You held my hand and helped me see...

You shared with me the Father's love;
and focused me on His Kingdom above.

My pain was deep; my spirit so "blue,"
but Joy returned with help from you.

You listened, my friend.
You heard my cries.
You reminded me of Satan's lies.

Thank you for your friendship true.
My heart is healing with thanks to you.

February 21, 2012

A Daughter's Prayer

February 2012

A mother's love is a gift to treasure.
It fills one's heart too full to measure.

I do not know my mother's love.
My heart is filled by God above.

My mother is a slave to sin;
Angry and bitter so deep within.

Her mind is now addled; she's deeply confused.
The anger she carries by Satan is used.

The pain she has caused me
so deep and so strong;
I'm working on forgiving.
I have been sooo long...

I'm tired and weary; I want to be free
to walk in your love, Lord
and help Mom to "see"...

To see the pain within my heart.
To be sorry for this
and to want "A New Start."

For Mom to say, "I'm sorry"
and, "Let's start again."
My heart would be full;
We'd finally be friends!

Memorial Day Meditation, 2013

Missionaries are Warriors too;
They are frontline in God's battles!
The Gospel is the saber/sword
That each so ably rattles!

They leave their homes and families,
to go and serve
just as you please.

Many battles are fought
as this war rages on...
Our enemy won't rest
'til the Gospel Message is gone!

BUT:

Jesus, you're our Captain.
You lead us in this fight.
The power is in your Spirit,
not in our strength or might.

You won this war upon the cross.
You gave your life for man.
We now can live eternally,
according to God's plan.

So let us each continue on,
to share the Gospel story.
To gather in the "Lost, now found"
and give you all the Glory!

M.C.

A Witness Bold and True

Let me be your witness;
Bold and pure and true.
Using every word I say
To point the way to You!

Let me live in such a way
That people see your face.
And I will tell them
of your love,
Your mercy and your grace.

Holy Spirit, fill my heart;
Pour in to "Overflow"!
Empower me
to preach your Word,
And to see your Kingdom grow!

Judy Williams, you've retired;
You've left us for good.
You're relaxing and renewing;
It is well that you should.

You spent so many years
With our tiniest tots;
Sharing your love
and hugging them lots!

The smiles you gave
Were as bright as the sun!
You've blessed so many lives;
I'm grateful to be one!

No more loyal a para,
a coworker, or friend,
Can anyone find from
Beginning to End.

As a grandma you shine,
As a mom you're the best!
No one could replace you;
You outshine the rest!

We're lonely without you
We miss you a lot!
In each of our hearts
you have a reserved spot!

So, as you begin
To "move on" to new things
Remember this moment
And all the love that it brings!

MC
Jan. 23, 2014

"Wait"

The word "Wait"
is the word you've given.
I'm listening, Lord
and by your Spirit I'm driven.

I'm driven to study
and to learn how to wait.
To hope and to trust
while I keep my path straight.

To focus on you, Lord
and those things from above:
Long-suffering, Patience,
Forgiveness, and Love.

My Hope is in you, Lord.
You are Faithful and True.
Walking always in Trust
is my promise to you!

Lord, bless this home
as we enter in.
Make it Holy
and free from sin.

Let our lives reflect
your mercy and grace.
May we discover your beauty
in each neighbor's face.

Keep our focus on you,
on your Kingdom above.
Fill our home with the blessings
of Laughter and Love

A Grandma's Prayer

Thank you, Lord, for this babe
in my arms.
Please bless her with gifts
of all Godly charms:

Patience, compassion, kindness
and love.
Wisdom, discernment of those
things from Above.

Place your hedge of protection
around this sweet child.
Protect and provide for her
in this world oh so wild!

Please meet all her needs
wherever she goes;
Enlighten her heart,
so her father she knows.

Let my prayers for Miss Emily
Stay 'round about your Throne;
And surround this sweet baby
so she's never alone.

Amen

A February Thought

Marian Colton

A new year starts; the months progress,
The days roll by; I must confess.

I've just put away my Christmas tree,
and Valentine Cards are staring at me...!

Reds and purples, mixed with pink.
Love and Romance abound, I think.

Who doesn't want to be surrounded by love?
Or to know that they are fondly thought of?

So, send a card or make a call...
Let someone know they're your "All in All."

It could be your family or "Just a friend."
This small act of Love is what matters in the end...

This Valentine's Day is a great time to show others that you care! It is also a good time to reconnect with those we may have "lost touch with..." Rekindling "cooled relationships" warms the heart. "Happy Valentine's Day!"

America's Keswick: A Place to Renew...

Marian Colton

I know a very special place,
With lakes, and grass, and sun.
It is a Godly, spiritual place,
offering fellowship and fun!

A place to laugh, and to sing God's praise,
To reflect and offer up prayer.
When you spend some time
and walk the grounds,
God's Presence meets you there!

"A place where God changes hearts,"
I've often heard it said...
Where One can leave worldly cares behind,
and look to Christ instead!

I thank you, Lord, for this place,
and for Your presence there.
You fill it with Your peace and joy,
and bless it with Your care!

This poem is written about America's Keswick, a Christian Conference Center many of us "locals" are familiar with. It is a Blessing to our community and to all who utilize its many resources!

My Quiet Place

Marian Colton

Sitting by the water's edge,
Savoring a breeze.
I'm listening for my Savior's voice
to tell me how to please...

To please You, Father,
and Your son,
the Holy Spirit—Three in One.

My prayers I offer
sincere and true,
Proclaiming my heartfelt
love for You!

Accept my praise
and daily prayer.
In my Quiet Place, Lord,
Come and meet me there.

As we celebrate the "Dog Days of Summer" spending time at the local beach (be it ocean, bay, or lake) and simply take in all of God's wondrous Creation, let's remember to offer up a quiet "Thank you" to the Creator Himself.

A Message from the Father

by Marian Colton

I go where God sends me and do what He says "Do";
I share His love with others and that surely includes you!

If you are reading this poem, I'm about to share with you
the Words of our Father that He is speaking to you.

"You are my very own, My greatest creation!
I rejoice over you with fatherly elation!"

"Remember that I love you; my son died for your sins.
When you come back to Me, a New Life in you begins!"

"So, come home to your Father, in the name of His Son;
Be Blessed by the Spirit that your 'New Life' has begun!"

As you celebrate with family and friends during these active summer months, consider the Father's love for each one of his children. He blesses us with the sun every morning and the moon each night. He waters our gardens with gentle summer rains and refreshes us with cooling breezes. As He showers us with all of these Blessings, perhaps we could pause and offer up a prayer of thanksgiving!

"Welcome back to a new school year!"
May it be successful and full of cheer.

May the Lord be first in all you do,
and may He keep His hand upon you!

Please know that you are in our daily prayer,
and about your "Mission" we truly care.

May each of your students truly take heed,
to the Word of God and follow your "lead"...

May God anoint every effort you take,
to transform lives and solid Christians to make!

The Prime Timers Ministry of Calvary Lighthouse
Welcoming back the teachers and staff of Calvary Academy.

Seasons Change...

Marian Cotton

Seasons change, and so do men.
Life never stays the same.
But Father God does not change;
Trusting Him should be our aim.

He's always there to hear our cries.
He listens to every prayer.
Then He works in us to "Do a Work,"
So His love we will "Go and share."

So, when you feel the winds of Change,
you have no need to fear...
The Love and Grace of Father God
with you are always near!

Our lives go through changes as do the seasons... May we allow the love
of God to warm our hearts during times of cold isolation or when the
winds of bitterness blow through our lives.

Autumn Harvests

by Marian Colton

We awaken to crisp, cool mornings and there are changes to the air.
We can't "identify" these differences; but our senses know they're there!

Fall is fast approaching; Harvest Time is here!
Chrysanthemums and pumpkins are seen both "far and near."

The Father's fields are also ready for His Harvest to begin.
I'm a laborer in this "Harvesting"; lost/hurting souls to bring in...

"The time is ripe to follow Christ, to live our lives for God.
He's waiting still with open arms, no matter from which road you've trod!"

As we experience the glorious autumn foliage and wrap ourselves in the warmth of a favorite sweatshirt or jacket, let us pause to give praise to the Creator of all the Blessings we experience in each and every season of our lives!

The Prayer of a Poet.

by Marian Colton

Lord, the poems I write are meant just for you;
but, "Share them with others" I so often do...

They're written to bring to You, honor and glory,
and to offer to others the Gospel story.

Please bless my paper and my pen,
That my words will touch the hearts of men.

May my words create a tiny spark,
that ignites a flame in hearts grown dark.

May the light of Your love shine bright in each heart!
And with those who've the "need" a relationship start.

May all those who read each poem I share,
Return to You, Lord, and also to prayer.

May this be the true "Thanksgiving Tradition"—That we each offer up a small "Thank you" to the one who created us all! May your homes be filled with the blessings of Peace, Hope, and Joy during this Happy Harvest Season! And may your cornucopias overflow with the fruits of Faith, Kindness, and Love! "Happy Thanksgiving!"

The Gifts You Give...

by Marian Colton

We gather today to celebrate, and to rest from all our labors;
Those many ways we volunteer in service to our neighbors!

The help you give all through the year is such a special gift!
It makes our Village a nicer place, and people's spirits do "Lift"!

You give of your time and energy with no thoughts of "Reward."
Your choice to share your life with others is "of your own accord."

We so appreciate the gifts you share with Village Six each day;
and pray that you are blessed by God in so very many ways!

So, "Thank you for your service, for all those things you do!
May this Season of 'Good Will Towards Men' pour out Blessings
over you!"

A Christmas Meditation

Marian Colton

We've strung the lights upon the tree;
the wreath is on the door...
Christmas Carols fill the air;
Our home is ready once more.

We wrap up gifts for family and friends;
We bake and mix and cook...
The time we spend on Christmas "prep"
Could fill the pages of a book!
BUT...
Let's not forget this Christmas Day,
That Jesus's birth was real.
Let's stop and pray "Happy Birthday!"
Both Joy and Peace we will feel.

So, "Happy Birthday, Jesus!"
I'll give these gifts to you:
I'll love my neighbor as myself,
and love You pure and true.

Merry Christmas to one and all! My personal prayer is that each and every one is blessed with good health, peace of mind, and a happy heart this Holiday season! Whether you celebrate Channukah, Kwanza, Christmas, or a Holiday I haven't named here, may your life be blessed with family and friends too numerous to count. May your 2018 be filled with God's blessings!

God's Christmas Gift...

Marian Colton

God's gift of Love has been passed down;
it began in a manger and poured forth from a thorny crown.
This love from our Father is meant for us all.
It shone forth on a cross but began in a stall.

In order to die, Christ had to be born.
To redeem us from sin, and from all shame and scorn.
Jesus's birth was so simple, so quiet and still...
In a stable so humble; prophesy to fulfill.

His birth we proclaim with much joy and praise!
Glory and honor we give to these days...
May our hearts carry over this glad jubilation
As we ponder the cross and Christ's gift of Salvation !

Snowmen and Sparrows

"He washes white as snow"
Words from a Hymn we often sing.
So, if you've chosen a snowman,
Let that thought in your own heart sing!

"He cares for the tiny sparrow."
How much more for you and me?
Each bird that you may have chosen,
reminds you that His love makes us free!

So, whichever your gift, let it always remind you
of God's Mercy and Grace and Love
with which He binds you!

This poem was presented with gifts to the Good News Team Members.
Christmas 2016

I will Listen; I Will Speak

Marian Colton

Lord, I'm in need of inspiration.
I'm not sure what to say.
So, I'll spend some time within Your Word.
I will listen; I will pray.

I will open up my heart to You.
I'll let your truths "sink in."
Then I'll know just what to share with folks,
Of love and grace and sin...

The words I speak are never "mine."
They all belong to You.
You bless me with inspired thoughts,
God-given, pure, and true.

So, I will speak
and I will share,
To let folks know
how much you care!

Your love for us
is strong and true.
That's why I live
my life for You!

We each have a friend who "sticks closer than a brother." If you are feeling lonely or isolated, a conversation with God does wonders! He speaks so clearly to us in His Word. The Bible is His Love Story to each one of us! We just have to open our hearts and listen...

"I Know in Whom I Believe."

Marian Colton

God is God and man is man.
The Lord can do what no man can!

He creates a sunset, pours down rain.
He upholds the weary, heals their pain.

He allays a fear, makes a weak man strong.
He listens to our prayers all the day long.

No man can do the work of God,
Upon this earth we daily trod...

For God, alone, can save my soul,
Forgive my sin and make me whole!

In God I trust and will believe,
His Grace and Mercy to receive.

For God is God and man is man.
The Lord can do what no man can!

As we enter a "New Era" with a new presidential administration; sadly; our nation's people are so very divided! Let's all try to remember that although we have differing political views, in the end we are all members of one race—the Human Race!

A Winter Evening's Meditation

by Marian Colton

The days are short and nights "drag on"...
The world is "hunkered in."
We have lots of time for reflective thoughts
of Love and Grace and sin,

Do I gossip, gripe, complain, or whine
whenever life gets rough?
Or do I sit before the Lord
in prayer, when times get tough?

The difference is amazing,
depending on my choice.
Joy and Peace will fill my heart
when I listen for His voice!

If I choose to gripe, complain and cry,
depression sets in and I'm not sure "Why"...
If I cry unto the Lord in prayer, I can rest assured
for He is with me there!

So, in my winter meditations
I'll take these thoughts away:
"That in all Life's trials and tribulations,
I will take the time to pray."

During these cold, long winter nights we can choose to be miserable or to be at peace. Our attitude often affects our "altitude" when it comes to our state of mind. May you each and all be blessed with peace and joy this winter as you reflect on God's love, grace, and mercies which are new every morning! May His love warm your hearts and your homes.

Every Day is a "New Adventure"...

by Marian Colton

Every day is a "New Adventure"
Walking with the Lord.
Facing trials and opportunities
prevents one from becoming bored.

With every sunrise life is new,
God's gift to us each day.
We awake with opportunities
to love, to serve, to pray...

Each day that we are given
Is another time to share
and to offer up to this big world
Our compassion, love, and care!

To speak of the Lord,
and of His love for all men.
To invite folks to "Come Home,"
and walk with Him again!

There is a famous saying, "Every day is a gift from God; that's why it is called the present." Let us each use our time wisely, living by the Golden Rule and loving one another as He has loved us! Let us also never forget to be thankful for each new day we are given!

His Faith in Me.

Marian Colton

I've suffered through a "silent time";
no words for "how I feel."
His love is true, of that I'm sure.
His faith in me is real.

He gives me space to grow and change,
My inner life to "rearrange."
But I wander off and lose my way.
Far from His Throne I often stray...

He only lets me get so far;
then His voice I hear to me call...
I'm drawn back close into his arms;
He will not let me fall!

I'm grateful for His trust in me,
And for His daily Grace.
I choose to live my life for Him
Until I see His face!

This poem was written after a "dry spell" that writers often experience. When the words flow again, it is like a refreshing dip in a cool spring. One feels rejuvenated! In each of our own lives, we can experience a "dry spell" in our relationships... But by reconnecting with old friends or getting out and making some new ones, we can each experience refreshing and renewal! If you feel you have no one, remember, God is always near!

A Safety Patrol Prayer

Marian Colton

We thank You, Lord, for those who care;
and with our Village their time they share.

They wait 'til its late...and at night they go out
to "check open garage doors,"
and what they're about...

If a streetlight is out, they "Call it in..."
So it can quickly be turned on again!

They care about
their friends and neighbors,
so they share with all, their dedicated labors!

While most are at home watching TV,
They're out and about
Monitoring the Village's safety.

So, as they patrol, Lord;
We ask you to bless them.
To "ride along side"
and with Your protection "caress" them.

Village Six Lighthouse Dedication Ceremony

August 4th, 2017

We gather today for a sweet Celebration:
Village Six's Safety Patrol Lighthouse Dedication.

This Safety Patrol Team is a dedicated Crew;
And here, on this day, Lord, we come before You.

We ask that you continue to bless them,
to protect and provide, and with safety caress them.

Be with each one as we take calls or we ride.
Look after our health and in peace may we abide.

As we serve all our neighbors with joy and in love,
Fill us each with your presence—a gift from above!

We dedicate this Safety Patrol Team to You,
And ask for Your blessings in all that we do.

Amen.
Marian Colton

September Song

by Marian Colton

School bells ring,
Cheer Squads sing,
Libraries are crowded.
Summer has passed,
but its memories will last,
although in "schedules" they may be clouded...
As Fall sets in
We all begin
to slow down and "settle in"...
Routines return,
but we all can learn
as we "look back to where we've just been"...
The things we've done,
in our summer fun,
Can help us to look ahead...
Joys we've shared.
"Attempts" we've dared;
Remove all fears and dread.
As September starts
Let's have open hearts
To learn from the things we've done...
To use our past
and move real fast
Into a future that's already begun!

With the opening of a new school year for our children and grandchildren, let's remember to keep them, their teachers, bus drivers, etc. in our daily prayers. Let's also keep in mind that one is never too old to learn something new! May we always look to be a blessing to others. Something we've learned from our past may just help someone's future!

October's Glory

by Marian Colton

The air is chill; the leaves are turning.
For a "Foliage trip" my heart is yearning...

To see the trees in all their glory;
As season's change, God shares His story.

I want to see and hear it all.
The sights and sounds that scream out, "It's Fall!"

Summer has gone; a new season's begun...
Fresh Glories to see; new races to run...

I'll savor each moment of this Glorious Fall,
and give thanks to the Lord who has created it all!

As we experience the change of seasons, we experience life in an exciting new and different way! Each season brings joys and challenges of its own. It is the same with the "seasons of our life." May the autumn of our lives bring us crisp, colorful memories that will carry us through the quiet, chilling stillness of a "snow-drifted winter"! Happy Harvest Time to all!

My "First Love"

by Marian Colton

To You, oh Lord, my heart belongs.
I write for you, my Poems and Songs.

I give to You my words of Praise,
and live for You each of my days.

You have my heart; that is for sure.
My love for You is both strong and pure.

This love I have can only be...
Because, dear Lord, You first loved me!

"For God so loved the world..." I for one am glad He did (and still does!). This Valentine's Day is a good day to reflect upon just how Faithful God has been to us! It's also a good day to share His love with others... Send a note or card to someone who needs uplifting. Even a phone call can make someone's day! Be someone's "Valentine"; you'll be blessed in return. "Happy Valentine's Day!"

A Mother's Day "Thank you."

by Marian Colton

Thank you, Mom, for all you do.
I love you very much!

God has blessed me with your tender care,
and special loving touch.

You've taught me how to hear God's Word,
and also how to pray.

You are God's special gift to me.
I thank Him every day!

To all Moms everywhere, living here or in the Heavenly realm,
"Happy Mother's Day!"

May your day be a blessing to you as you are to your children!

A Memorial Day Thought

by Marian Colton

We thank You, dear Lord, for those who have served
to protect this great nation and its freedom preserved.

Those who have given their lives, deserve our respect.
And giving tribute to them we should never neglect!

So, as we each celebrate this Memorial Day,
Let us pause to reflect and for Peace let us pray!

As we look to Memorial Day as the official start of summer, let us also stop and remember all those who've given their lives in the service of their country! Happy Memorial Day, and to all veterans we say, "Thank you for your service!"

Ponderings from My Sunporch...

by Marian Colton

I'm sitting here on a sunny day,
for some "Quiet Time" to think and to pray,

I'm not alone, Lord, You're with me here.
You grant me peace and remove all fear!

Your love is deep, and wide, and strong.
It refreshes me all day long!

In You I put my faith and trust.
As a Child of God, this is a "must"!

You gave Your life so I'd be free;
to live with You eternally.

So, as I sit in this "Quiet place,"
I thank You for Your Amazing Grace!

As we begin to spend more time outdoors and in nature, let us take time to reflect on God's love for us! Creation sings of His glory! Just listen to wild birdsongs or inhale the fragrance of lilies and honeysuckle. Capture the sight of a herd of deer or flock of wild turkeys as they roam through a local meadow... Creation "screams out" thankfulness to a Creator! I will do the same! Perhaps you will join me...?

Use Me, Lord, to Sing Your Song

by Marian Colton

You, oh Lord, have made me whole.
Jesus's life You offered for my soul.

I am no longer a slave to sin.
A sanctified life, I choose to begin!

To follow Your ways, Lord, is my desire.
Ignite my spirit with Your Holy Fire!

I'll sing Your praises wherever I go,
And share of Your Gospel so others will know...

Please help me and guide me along Life's long way;
Protect and provide as I go through each day.

Let my life be an instrument playing Your song,
And my words sing the melody clearly and strong!

I have made it my mission to share with others my faith, hope, and joy in my relationship with the Lord. I hope that I share these attributes with each of you as well! They are "there for the taking!" God's gifts to us each day. We just have to receive the gift and accept it from the Giver! Have a Happy 4th of July, and may God Bless America!

I Will Share...

by Marian Colton

The love You give, Lord, is the love I'll share
With every person everywhere.

I'll tell of Your mercy and share of your grace;
I'll listen to their heart, Lord, as I "study" each face.

I will intercede in heartfelt prayer,
To share with each, Your loving care.

I'll lay their needs before Your throne,
So each heart will know it is not alone.

I will praise Your name and give You glory,
And share with all the Salvation story!

I'll pray they give their hearts to You,
That their Joy be full their whole lives through!

As I walk with the Lord, I find myself blessed with such Peace, Hope, and Joy that I want others to experience these gifts as well! The words "See something, say something..." aren't just for bad things. I see the goodness and the faithfulness of the Lord every day! I must say something so others' eyes (and hearts) may be opened to see it too! "Seek and you shall find!"

Two simple Words

by Marian Colton

"Thank you" are two simple words; but they say so very much!
They offer up appreciation for all the lives you touch.

The time that you spend on behalf of your neighbors
is a blessing to all who are touched by your "labors."

Whether checking garage doors or calling in broken lights,
You're sharing your time and giving up nights.

We never have to wait for the Chatter;
Your timely delivery really does matter!

When the food truck arrives, it's "All hands on deck!"
You help park the cars so there's never a wreck!

The help that you all give, we honor today.
And the Blessings of God for you each do we pray!

I Give This Day to You...

by Marian Colton

Oh Lord, I give this day to You.
Be part of all I say and do.

Surround me with Your Love and Grace,
That I may bring them every place!

May my smile shine with Your precious light,
That I might offer Hope so bright!

Let my every thought be centered on others...
My neighbors and friends, all my "sisters and brothers."

As I live my life, let me offer Your love,
and encourage reflection on Heaven above!

I want my life to put forth Your Glory,
and for each of my words to tell of your story.

How You lived and died for each woman and man,
to fulfill the Father's Salvation plan!

My "Mission" in life is to share my faith with others and to remind people that they have a Father Who loves them. So many folks are alone and isolated from family and friends. Sometimes a simple smile or "Good morning!" spoken by a neighbor can brighten up their day! These little "niceties" are God's way of letting us know that we really do matter! Let's all "get our smiles on" and encourage one another!

The Legacy of a Life Well Lived...

by Marian Colton

Aunt Jenny, today we bid you "Farewell"
we say our "Final Goodbye."

We thank God for the life that you lived so well,
and for knowing that your life did not end when you died.

The Legacy you've left is both living and strong!
Your Joy and your Strength still carry us along.

You are now in the place of Eternal Rest, a place of unspeakable Peace!
we celebrate your life and the love that you've shared;
your Legacy will never cease!

This tribute was read at Aunt Jenny's Memorial Ceremony, following Chris's prayer and directly before Rich dispensed Jenny's ashes into the inlet directly below Barnegat Lighthouse ("Old Barney" as Jenny liked to refer to it). The day was sunny, with deep blue skies and the water was filled with life! Boaters, fishermen, families out to "climb to the top of 'Old Barney,'" strolled the sands and seawall... The perfect day for Jenny's "Homeward Bound Journey"!

8/12/2018

An Autumn Reflection...

by Marian Colton

The winds of change begin to blow,
as Autumn colors all around us glow....

Leaves turn from green to crimson and gold;
Soft breezes from warm, to chilly and bold!

Days are shorter and nights grow long.
Summer fades as Autumn grows strong!

Seasons change; it must happen, I fear.
We cannot stop it; it's the same every year...

As the seasons change, so does life.
We live through "seasons of joy" and "seasons of strife."

BUT:

Whatever the season of Life you are in,
You can turn to the Lord, and a New Life begin!

Winter, Spring, Summer, or Fall,
Our Father is waiting for you to give Him your all!

As I go through the various stages of my life, I treasure the faithfulness of God more and more! Each season has its trials, but also its "treasures." Sometimes one must go through one to get to the other... May the glories of this autumn season fill your heart to overflow with peace, hope, and joy!

Grateful...

by Marian Colton

I spent my youth far from God;
I'm ashamed to recall some of the roads that I've trod...
But shame has no place in my thinking today.
I'm forgiven, redeemed, and in gratitude I pray...

I thank the Lord for saving my soul,
Forgiving my sins and making me whole!
He does the same for every person who asks.
Forgiveness of sins was one of Christ's tasks.

The other was to share our Father's great love,
And swing open the gates to Heaven above!
So, no matter what you've said or done,
You can turn to Christ—the Holy One.

He will change your heart as He changed me,
So you can live with God eternally!
These are reasons to be grateful,
To be more kind and much less hateful!

Let go of grudges, let anger fall away...
Forgive and forget; and for others do pray!

Happy Thanksgiving! May your heart and your home be filled with an Attitude of Gratitude. We each have so much to be thankful for! God's Creation surrounds us, and He fills our lives with friends and family to share Life with. If you know someone who is alone or feeling down, perhaps you can share a smile or kind word with them. It will make their day!

The Christmas Story

by Marian Colton

The most beautiful story that I've ever heard
Is the Nativity Story from God's Holy Word.

"No room in the Inn," a stable for his birth.
Such a humble, lowly "Welcome" to the Savior of the Earth!

Jesus was born and placed in a manger.
The Wise Men searched for him in spite of great danger!

They had faith he was coming; so they followed the star...
To worship their Messaiah, though the journey was far.

The Angels proclaimed him to shepherds in fields;
"Joy to the World!" Emmanuel's presence yields.

Both shepherds and Kings went to the stable.
Each bowed down to their Lord and gave gifts as they were able...

We still can give gifts to our Savior today,
I offer to him all I do and all I say.

The gift that God gave to us that first Christmas morn,
Was that in order to die for us; Christ had to be born!

So, as you retell the Nativity Story:
Reflect on Salvation and give God all Glory!

The wood of the manger is so "tied in to the wood of the cross!" Jesus had to be born in order to sacrifice his life for the forgiveness of our sin... "What a precious gift!" God loves each one of us THAT much! This Christmas, as you are listening to your favorite Christmas carols, remember that our Heavenly Father waits for us to open His gift to us, "For God so loved the world that He gave His only begotten son; that whoever believes in him shall not perish but have eternal life." John 3:16

YOU HONOR OUR SOLDIERS;
THE HUNGRY YOU FEED,
YOU SPEND YOUR LIFE
HELPING ALL OTHERS IN NEED.

YOU DO YOUR WORK QUIETLY;
NO FAME AND NO GLORY.
SERVICE TO OTHERS
IS YOUR PERSONAL LIFE STORY.

THE "STORM OF THE CENTURY"
SLAMMED INTO YOUR LIFE.
IT RESULTED IN CHAOS
WHICH COULD CAUSE ANXIETY AND STRIFE.

BUT YOUR FAITH STANDS YOU STRONG.
YOUR HEART REMAINS TRUE.
THIS "BUMP IN THE ROAD"
WILL NOT DEFEAT YOU!

YOU'LL REBUILD AND YOU'LL HEAL; YOUR JOY WILL
RETURN.
AS YOU RECOVER FROM SANDY;
HIS LIGHT OF LOVE IN YOU BURNS!

YOU'VE SET THE EXAMPLE;
YOU ARE A DEAR FRIEND.
LET OUR OFFERINGS OF LOVE
"SEE YOU THROUGH" AND HELP YOU "MEND"

My Gift to You...

by Marian Colton

My gift, dear friend, is a daily prayer,
that God keep you safe in His tender care.

May you grow in strength and in His power,
And may you "Dance in the puddles of His 'Blessings Shower'!"

I look to the Lord and seek His face,
As I ask Him to pour out His Mercy and Grace.

I ask God to send you "Blessings galore"...
and as you tally them up, I pray He sends more!

This prayer was written for my dear friend's seventy-fifth birthday. The joy on her face as she received it is engraved in my memory forever! As we begin the New Year of 2019, let's make it our "Mission" to lift up each other in prayer. It couldn't hurt. I personally believe it will drastically help! As we pray for one another, perhaps we will open ourselves to new relationships, new adventures, and new levels of communication with one another! Happy New Year! May 2019 be your "Best year ever!"

Two Gifts That We Give...

Marian Colton

Sharing and Caring are two gifts that we give
To our friends and our neighbors in this place where we live.
We check out each home most every night,
To check that garage doors are "closed up tight."
So neither "man nor beast" can enter in;
and folks are safe in their home within.
We're checking streetlights along the way;
If they're "out," it's reported right away!
We deliver the Chatter in the rain, wind, and snow;
So our neighbors stay connected and "kept in the know"...
We gladly help out on "Food Truck Day,"
Which is a blessing to all; we hope and we pray...
But....
It's more than the doors, Much more than the Chatter...
We're telling our neighbors that they really do matter!
These gifts that we give are given with love;
and the person who sends us is the Lord up above!
As Hannukah and Christmas are each drawing near,
This is a "Reflective" time of year...
A time to thank God for all that you do,
And to ask for His blessings over each one of you!

This poem was written and presented to the Crestwood Village Six Safety Patrol members at their Holiday Breakfast held in December. The appreciation it extols extends to all Volunteers of every Village serviced by the *Crestwood Sun* newspaper! People who serve their neighbors and friends in any capacity deserve our prayers and support! The "Life" of a community depends upon its members participation. So, "Thank you" to all who share of their time, talent, and tenacity to keep our Villages "rolling along"... Happy Valentine's Day!

The "Spice of Life"

by Marian Colton

The time I spend in daily prayer is time well spent with You.
It prepares me to "Walk through the day," as it "flavors" what I do!

Prayer "seasons" all I say, with Wisdom and with Light,
that my words encourage all my friends, and makes their day more bright!

As I "sprinkle" prayer throughout my day, it enhances all I do...
"Spicing up" each simple act to point the way to You!

I consider Prayer "the Spice of Life"; and I use it every day;
to flavor everything I do and to "season" all I say.

So keep this "Spice Jar" handy, and know it's always there
to sprinkle on your troubles or over those for whom you care.

In this month of Valentine's Day, let's remember to "share the Love"
with friends and family! I find that a great way to show you care is to
let someone know that you're keeping them lifted up in prayer! It tells
them that they are important to you and that you are thinking of them.
So, with your Valentine cards and notes, share a prayer or two; it costs
nothing yet is "priceless!"! Happy Valentine's Day!

March

by Marian Colton

The month of March is a curious thing;
it isn't strong Winter, but not yet quite Spring...
It "Comes in like a lion, but goes out like a lamb."
It is windy and chilly; often thunderstorms "slam!"

Some folks say, "There isn't much to do,"
But I have some thoughts to share with you:
Perhaps send a note or call on a friend.
You'd both be happier in the end...

Or, open up a book to read;
Both mind and spirit it would feed.
I choose the Bible to read for myself,
and Keep one handy on my bookshelf.

If you can't read a book or cannot write a letter,
Here's an idea that might suit you better:

You can sit back in your chair and reflect, praise, and pray
for all whom you care for or "connect with" each day!
Praying for people is a healthy thing to do...
It benefits others and brings blessings upon you!

So, if "the ides of March" start to "bring you down,"
choose an item from my list and trade a smile for your frown!

Time Well Spent...

by Marian Colton

Time in prayer is time well spent; to God it draws me near...
The time I spend can improve my mood or take away my fear.

I talk with God about many things. It's a lengthy conversation...
We speak of friends and family, the world, my church, this nation,

The Bible is "The Word of God"; where He speaks to me so clearly.
He answers every prayer I pray and draws me close so "dearly."

God shares with me His eternal love and helps me through each day.
He tells me how to improve my life and guides me in how to pray.

The Word of God speaks to my heart; I must "quiet down" to hear...
"Be still and know that I am God" (Psalm 46:10) are words I hold so dear!

So, if you'd like to live this year "opening yourself to prayer,"
Begin to read the Word of God and start the practice there!

Everyone needs someone to talk to. I have found that God is a very
good Listener! When I need someone to lean on, no one does it better!
Prayer is my best weapon against fear, depression, anger, and bitterness!
I highly recommend it! In any situation I find myself, I look to Him
first, and I've never been disappointed! "Try it. You might like it."

Victory!

by Marian Colton

The battle is over; the war has been won!
It ended on Calvary with the death of God's son.

Jesus went to the cross and he died for our sin,
to offer forgiveness and to let Redemption begin!

He rose in three days holding the keys to Salvation.
When we believe and receive him, we become a New Creation!

Some are still "Stuck in the battle" and are "Lost in the fray,"
They haven't accepted Christ's gift to this day...

Salvation, Forgiveness, Mercy, and Love,
Are the "spoils" of Christ's Victory poured forth from Above!

So, if you're weary of the battle and want to "leave the fray"
Accept Christ's Gift of Salvation and live for him today!

Spring—New Life! It's a time for New Beginnings and Fresh Starts...
I can't think of a better time to pause, reflect, and to make the decision
to renew my relationships with others and with God!

An Ode to the Son...

by Marian Colton

We gather together to pray in your name.
To thank you for your blessings and for "Not casting blame"...

You forgive what we do when we truly repent;
As you pour out God's Grace, for it's by Him you were sent!

You hung on the cross, paid the price for our sin.
Your arms still spread "open wide" to welcome us in!

You've given to us a much-treasured gift, but we must each believe it.
We must open our hearts to God's Salvation plan and faithfully receive it.

Easter has "Come and gone..." but the relevance of the "Empty Tomb" continues on! It is never too late to "resurrect" our relationship with our Creator! The Lord always has room for one more in His Kingdom! May your Memorial Day be one of reflection of the sacrifices made on your behalf, especially that of Christ on the cross.

Two Days in May

by Marian Colton

Two days in May we pause to recall
the people who share with others and "Give their all!"

Mother's Day, a time for honoring Moms is reserved.
Memorial Day we parade for Fallen Heroes who have served.

Each give of themselves to care for all others;
Brave men and brave women and also our mothers!

To each we owe our gratitude; They've sacrificed so much!
So, pray for them and thank the Lord for all the lives they touch.

Let us each set aside time to reflect upon all the sacrifices made on our behalf. Moms who loved and cared for us, as well as those men and women who sacrificed their very lives so that we may live in Freedom! May you each have a Happy Mother's Day and a Blessed, Happy Memorial Day!

My Choice

by Marian Colton

Lord, I sit in quiet stillness listening for Your voice.
My life in You, dear Father, affords me no such other choice.

I've left "the World" and all it's "charms," though it often "Calls to me."
So much of it is the "evil" from which you've set me free!

I've made a choice to live for You; You are my Lord and King,
I live my life within Your Word; and I give you my "everything!"

Everything I think and say, all that I choose to do...
The choices that I make each day, begin and end in You!

June is the sixth month on our calendar. We are halfway through to the end of another year! It is a good time to slow down and "take stock" of our lives. If we need to make any changes, NOW is as good a time as any... Remember, God is only a prayer away!

God Has Blessed America...

by Marian Colton

I like to hear the bird's songs each and every day,
to listen to the squirrels "talk" as they romp and scamp and play!

The languages of Creation are as vast as they are strong.
They help to keep me "centered" and soothe me all day long...

They also keep me focused on God's gifts to us each day,
and remind me of His presence for which I gratefully say:

"Thank You, Lord, for Your Creation!
And for placing me in this great nation!"

"Happy Birthday, America! I want to honor you,
to also thank the Lord above for the life I live in you!"

"God bless America, land that I love..." As you enjoy the coming summer activities, travel this nation's roadways, and celebrate the "fruits" of plentiful harvests, please take the time to pause and reflect upon "the Giver of All Good Gifts"... God bless each of you! Happy Summer!

Birds of a Feather...

by Marian Colton

"Birds of a Feather flock together" is how the saying goes...
As I watch my feeders every day, my faith in this fact grows.

So many birds arrive in flocks, while others come in pairs.
The ones who arrive all by themselves are greeted with "chirps and stares."

The solo birds eat and fly away,
While flocks and pairs will romp and play!

I feel like we are like these birds,
With our actions and our words,

We tend to stick with "our own kind,"
and pay those "others" never mind...

But if we'd open our hearts to someone "new,"
Perhaps we'd develop a friendship or two!

Opening one's heart to new people can be unsettling, especially if they look or speak differently than we do... But the rewards can be so gratifying! I am amazed at how many different species of birds share a meal at my bird feeders each day, and what a Symphony of Birdsong they produce together!

The Life-Breath of God

by Marian Colton

You created me in my mother's womb;
Your breath has brought me Life.

Let everything I say and do
Resound with Joy not strife!

May I live a life that points to You
and gives your name all Glory!

Because You've breathed Your life into me,
I want to share your story:

How Your son gave his life upon a cross, so I'd be saved from my sins.
And as I repent and turn back to You, a New Life in me begins!

"Adopted In..."

by Marian Colton

In the stillness and the quiet I listen for Your voice.
I am Your child, oh Abba Father; I've made Your love my choice.

In church on every Sunday, In Your Scriptures every day.
In prayer "most every moment"; at work, at home, at play.

My life I live "As unto You"; Your purpose to fulfill.
I live according to Your Word; and surrender to your will!

So, use me, Lord and anoint my works to be a blessing to others...
That they might give their hearts to you and become my sisters and brothers!

I've given my heart to the Lord; it is something I've never regretted. If you've never thought about it, I highly recommend doing so! I like to say that since giving my heart to the Lord, "every day is a New Adventure!"

Those Who Serve

by Marian Colton

We talk a lot about "Those Who Serve," those who train to do what's right.
But there are those right here at home "Who serve with all their might."

These folks deserve a "Thank you," and much appreciation.
They are the strength of our communities, and the "Backbone of our nation!"

Today we gather as the Safety Patrol of Crestwood Village Six.
We donate our time and our energies; a dedicated mix!

Our neighbors we serve both night and day, in an effort to keep life good.
We do these things because we care, and understand that we should.

So, "Thank you for all the help you give to our Community.
It makes our lives more pleasant to live, and we thank you gratefully!"

This poem was written as a tribute to those who serve on Crestwood Village Six's Safety Patrol. These men and women continually "put others first"; they give up time, energy, and their own needs to meet the needs of their neighbors and acquaintances within the village. Their selflessness is an inspiration! Perhaps you are looking for some way to "get involved"? This team is always looking for new members. They are a joyful group of volunteers and would be happy to include you in their ranks!

Thanksgiving Day Reflections

by Marian Colton

I smell the turkey cooking;
I've already baked the bread.
As I prepare Thanksgiving dinner,
the Lord "is in my head..."

All the food that will fill my table,
the Lord has given to me.
He's also blessed my home today
with friends and family!

The foliage out my window
is so pleasing to my sight;
my heart is filled with gratefulness;
so I'll praise with all my might!

"Thank You, Lord, for my family and friends,
and for Your faithful love,
which never ends!"

"Thank You also for Your Salvation Plan;
It's the greatest gift
You've ever given to Man!"

This Thanksgiving, may each one of us offer up prayers of thanksgiving to "the Founder of our Feast"! Living with an Attitude of Gratitude not only blesses the Father; it inspires others to do the same. "Happy Thanksgiving! May the abundance on your table be only surpassed by the thankfulness in your heart!"

Harvest Time

by Marian Colton

As trees are changing colors, and the air begins to "chill,"
My heart beats a bit faster, and my soul gets such a "thrill!"

The sounds of crunching leaves falling on my ears,
has lifted my spirit higher for "oh so many years!"

A warm sip of coffee as I wander about,
is a treat that causes my heart to cry out!

"It's Harvest time; our labors are done!"
It's true for the Farmers, as well as God's son...

Christ finished his work on Resurrection Day;
He's still reaping His harvest 'til this very day!

"The Harvest is ready, but the laborers are few..." God is always looking for those who would share His love with others. This Thanksgiving, let's share His grace, love, and mercy with all those around us! After all, He blesses us in order that we can be a blessing to others! "Happy Thanksgiving!"

The Reason for the Season

by Marian Colton

Let each gift that we're given this Holiday Season,
Point to Christ's birth and why his life "had a reason."

Jesus's birthday is special; that fact is surely true!
He was born to give up his life, both for me and for you.

"Born to die," in fulfillment of his Father's plan.
He atoned for our sins, reconciling God the Father with Man!

Christ was born in a manger; "No room in the inn..."
Like the state of our hearts when we're "living in sin."

So, let's each open our heart to allow Christ to enter...
He will gift us with a New Life with God at its center!

"Unwrap the gift of Jesus" this Christmas Day!
Let him live in your heart, and "Gift" God with your life, I pray.

Jesus is truly "the Reason for the Season!" He needed to be born so that he could sacrifice his life as atonement for our sins! His death and resurrection is the greatest gift that has ever been given! It is God's gift of Love, Grace, and Mercy to each one of us! My prayer is that you "believe it and receive it" this Christmas! Blessings in the New Year 2020!

New Year's Day Reflections...

by Marian Colton

With the start of each New Year we pause and look within...
We "take stock" of where we're going, and the "places we have been".

"Am I living in a selfish place? Or do I sacrifice for others?"
"Do I strive for fame and glory? Or encourage my sisters and brothers?"

The Father has a plan for me, a path for me to travel.
But if I get distracted, this plan will swiftly unravel!

I must remain focused and remain in His Word,
and pray with true faith that my prayers will be heard.

Our Father is faithful; His love is sure and true!
A new year is beginning, and He is calling out to you:

"I'm your father: I love you. My son paid the price for your sin.
So give to me your heart and let your 'New Life in Me' begin!"

A New Year is a great time to reflect on our lives and to make any changes we deem necessary. The best change I ever made was to give my heart to the Lord and follow His will for my life. I've never been happier! My prayer is that 2020 bring you this same joy! Happy New Year!

"My Valentine"

by Marian Colton

"Will you be my Valentine? I'll give my heart to You.
You've given to me all you have, and your faithfulness is true!

Your gift of Love so long ago still blesses me today;
Jesus gave his life upon the cross, for my sin and shame "to pay."

You gave to me the gift of Life, Your mercy and Your grace.
How could I not return this love, and rightfully take my place?

I'll take my place around Your throne and worship at Your feet;
When I get home to "Glory," and Jesus I will meet!

Valentine's Day is a day of sharing loving thoughts with others. I make it a point to share my love with our Heavenly Father as well. His love is unconditional, eternal, and is for each one of us! So, if you are feeling a bit lonely on this Valentine's Day—Remember this: "Your Heavenly Father loves you 'to the moon and back!'" Happy Valentine's Day!

Three Days...

by Marian Colton

You were nailed to and hung upon Calvary's cross;
the disciples lived through the pain of Your "loss."

Each felt the sharp sting of loneliness;
they didn't understand Your Holiness.

They "allowed in" Doubt, and "courted" Fears,
although you had lived with them for those three years!

You allowed them to wait for three long days,
to see You rise and to sing Your praise!

Those three long days gave them each a choice,
To "Walk away" or "Listen for Your voice."

We live today with that same chance,
To walk away, or in Faith, advance...

Good Friday to Easter is still three days;
Time for reflection, prayer, and to offer you praise!

Three days it took for Your New Life to begin,
for Redemption to happen, and our cleansing from sin!

This Easter, I hope and pray that you each experience the love of God in a very real, personal, joyous way! May thoughts of Jesus's sacrifice for us put desires to be a blessing to others in our hearts. "May you each be blessed; that you may be a blessing to others!" "Happy Easter!"

Memorials Mean Something...

by Marian Colton

In the month of May we honor our Mothers;
they've invested in our lives so much more than most others!

Our Military too, we honor and praise!
Specifically those who "sacrificed their days."

We've set aside a day for each, to offer them our gratitude.
A Memorial Day is appropriate, along with our grateful attitude!

The Father gave us each, both the soldiers and our mothers.
Let us memorialize our thanks to Him by loving our Sisters and Brothers!

Memorials mean something. They show our thanks and love!
We share them with our fellow man, so why not with the Lord above?

This May, as we show gratitude to moms and military families who have
sacrificed so much on our behalf, let us remember the Father's sacrifice
of His only begotten son for the salvation of our souls! Perhaps a fitting
memorial would be to "Love one another as I have loved you" John
15:12.

A Love Letter...

by Marian Colton

I am your Lord; I am your Savior.
Loving you to good behavior…
I am there with you in each dark place,
Showering you with My love and grace.

I patiently wait for your every prayer.
Where you call out to Me, I will meet you there...
I love to spend My time with you!
To comfort, counsel, and "See you through..."

I want you to set your sights on Me.
To see My hope, not your anxiety.
What you need is what I give,
Strength, and hope, and the power to live!

So, come to me and take My hand.
Your faith and prayers can heal this land.
Though its sins are many and they are great;
With faith and prayer, it is never too late!

Listen to these words I say,
"Have faith in God and pray, pray, pray!"

During this time of self-distancing and isolation, many people are asking a lot of questions. I find that remembering that there is a place to turn for reassurance and peace helps to keep me grounded. Rather than focusing on fear and the "unknown" down the road, I look around at all of my daily Blessings and express gratitude. "Each new day is a gift; that is why it is called the present!" Please know that we are alone in this, TOGETHER!

Thank You for My Senses.

by Marian Colton

I look around and see the trees,
large flocks of birds, some bugs and bees.

I feel the warming rays of sun,
the breeze and all the "drafts" it's spun.

I hear the sound of children's play;
My heart feels so "at peace today!"

The smell of lilacs and honeysuckle sweet,
fill my nostrils; "What a treat!"

I share an apple with a friend. The taste is crisp yet sour.
It stirs my taste buds wide awake and restores my inner power.

My senses have all come alive! I'm grateful for each one.
Thank You, Lord, for blessing me with Life and Breath in Your Son!

The Lord sees what is happening. He hears all our prayers.
He tastes our Joy's sweetness, and can smell all of our fears.

He feels all our pain and shares in our sorrow;
So he offers to us Life and Hope for tomorrow!

As we have been "self-isolating" for such a long time, many of us have been communing with Nature a bit more so than usual. We have taken the time to savor the simpler things in life, to slow down and truly appreciate all the gifts we've been given! The warmth of the sun, the refreshment of a cool breeze. Even the joy of a tasty piece of fresh fruit! May we also enjoy the smile and wave of a neighbor as they "putter around their garden" or the kind "Hello!" shouted from passers-by.... May we emerge from this crisis a more Kinder, Gentler people... and "May God Bless America!"

Consolation in Our Isolation

by Marian Colton

The time that we've spent in Quarantine,
Has given us "Gifts" that perhaps we've not seen...

We've had time to do those "put-off chores"...
To read some books, and to scrub the floors!

The time to call or to write a letter...
To "reconnect" helped us each feel better!

As Life "Locked-down," we took it slow;
We learned some things and began to grow.

We've learned to better appreciate each other,
and perhaps lend a hand to a sister or brother!

The last few months have been quite different than usual! While they have been challenging, they've also provided many Blessings! My prayer is that you have remained healthy and perhaps experienced and embraced those Blessings bestowed upon us on a daily basis! May your summer season be one of peace, joy, and Hope for the Future!

Having Fun in the Summer Sun

by Marian Colton

The beaches are open and so are the lakes.
The sun is still shining, and boats still make "wakes"!

Breezes still blow; gardens still bloom!
Life is still happening outdoors, or in your room.

The taste of iced coffee still stirs my soul...
Life is worth living and enjoying it is my goal!

So, I'll pack up a lunch and head out to a park,
To hike, fish, or swim and "hang out" until dark!

I'll listen to birds, and enjoy each warm breeze.
I'll remember these gifts as I fall to my knees...
and say, "Thank You, Lord!"

So much of our "normal" summertime activities have been canceled or redesigned! However, some of Nature's most abundant blessings are still readily available! So, try getting outside to enjoy the abundance around you! May August's "Dog Days of Summer" "bark up the right tree" for you and yours!

A Day Full of Gifts!

by Marian Colton

I love to sing His praises, lift up my voice in song.
I thank the Lord for His gifts to me; He presents them all day long...

When I awake, He greets me through birdsongs sweet and trill,
As sunshine pours through windows, and breezes my curtains fill!

As morning fades to midday, my garden flowers "Call";
They need a bit of water so He "Showers" them one and all!

The richness of their colors and also of their scent;
Displays His love for nature and makes His presence evident!

As daylight fades and night has come, I look up to see a star.
It shines its light upon my yard from oh, so very far!

He set this world in motion, placed the stars up in the sky,
The birds to sing, and everything to praise the Lord Most High!

"Let everything that has breath, praise the Lord." Psalm 150:6. I am of the belief that saying "Thank you" is not only polite but is the right thing to do when a gift has been given to me. I have been given so very many! How about you...?

An Ode to Autumn

By Marian Colton

The crunch of leaves beneath my feet is a sound I'm happy to hear.
And as the scent of "logs upon a fire" drifts by, my love of Autumn shines clear!

I watch a flock of geese fly by in their usual "V" formation...
These "Signs of Fall" are more to me Testimonials to Creation!

Each miracle of Nature has been given by the Lord.
Experiencing and savoring them has been my heart's reward!

The treasures of this season, crisp air and foliage bright,
Sing out the praises of the Lord and shine out His Glorious Light!

He gives us gifts in each new season;
His love for us is His only reason...

So, I'll cherish these gifts with a grateful attitude,
And offer to God my prayers of gratitude.

With summer behind us and autumn's glory "falling in...", I am filled
with joy! I love this time of year! The colors, scents, and sounds of fall
"sing out to the Glory of God!" As you listen to Autumn's Song, may
your heart be filled as well. "Happy Harvest Season to you all!"

"True Thanksgiving"

by Marian Colton

We've set aside a Day of Thanks: it happens each November...
The Lord has blessed us in so many ways; it is right to pause and remember.

To remember our Blessings and all that we share.
We have a world full of wonder and a father who cares!

As birds fill the air and fish swim in the sea:
Mammals and insects fill the lands around me!

My eyes see such colors! My ears are filled with sounds!
Gratefulness for God's gifts to us, within my heart abounds!

I'm grateful for my senses, for music, art, and song...
For family, love, and friendship, and God's forgiveness of my "Wrong."

So, I will take this day to offer God "Thanksgiving,"
to praise His name and appreciate the life I have been living!

This Thanksgiving it is more important than ever to "count our Blessings!" With so much uncertainty surrounding us, let's look to the Blessed Assurance of the Father's love! "Happy Thanksgiving; have a blessed day! May this Holiday Season fill your heart with Faith, Hope, and Love!"

A Sweet Time of Prayer

by Marian Colton

Whenever I enter a sweet time of prayer,
I am never alone; for the Lord meets me there.

He listens intently to hear what I say.
His answer is forthcoming even as I still pray!

Before I speak it, He knows what I need.
And in the soil of my heart, He often "Plants a seed."

He plants within me seeds of faith, hope, and love,
Showering these seeds with power from Above!

The time I spend in prayer does me good.
It keeps me living as I should

Spending time with God in prayer.
Uplifts my soul and keeps it there!

Sometimes we just need to "talk to someone"... I have found that God is always a very good listener! As I share my heart with Him, He shares His love with me! May you be blessed this Thanksgiving with enough seeds to plant a garden of Faith, Hope, and Love!

This "Christmas Gift"...

by Marian Colton

I will be Your Witness.
I will go to where you send...
To share with ALL, Your love for us;
from the Beginning 'til the End:

His birth was in a stable
so lowly, meek, and mild...
You declared your steadfast love for us
through the wailings of a child.

"Born to die," it is often said
as the reason for his birth.
He lived his life to share with us
our value and our worth.

Upon the cross he sacrificed
His life to set us free,
that as we believe and accept this gift,
we'll receive Eternity!

This "Christmas Gift" You gave us
is an "Easter Gift" as well...
The sacrifice of Jesus's life
has rescued me from Hell!

This Christmas, I am reflecting upon the Greatest Gift I've ever been given! May your heart be open to receive this precious treasure as well! It truly is the "Gift that keeps On Giving!" Merry Christmas and Blessings in the New Year!

Happy New Year!

by Marian Colton

Twenty Twenty has "Come and gone"; it was a time of isolation.
A time for deep reflection and for in-depth meditation.

Some folks were sad, some were afraid. All felt a bit of tension...
As we enter into this brand New Year; we are filled with apprehension.

"Will they develop a vaccine or a cure? Will Therapeutics be found?
Will our businesses reopen? Will the Economy be sound?"

So many "What ifs" and doubts abound; the answers are "Up in the air!"
We nervously look to the future... But, relax; God is already there!

He's the God of Yesterday and Today... "Tomorrow?"... He is there too!
When you're anxious or scared, remember this:
He is the Father Who cares for You!

He has held our hand throughout this time.
He's provided for our every need.
He'll be with us in Twenty Twenty-One; our hungering hearts He will feed!

So, let your heart be hopeful. Celebrate this brand New Year!
Put your hand in the hand of the Father,
and move forward without doubts or fear!

This past year, so many unanswered questions have been swirling around in our brains! For just a moment or two, pause and reflect on all of those "Unexpected Blessings" you experienced this past year. Look forward to the New Year with a sense of expectancy and renewed hope! "Happy New Year!"

If You Need a Valentine...

by Marian Colton

Let every heart be open to the care sent from Above.
Our Father knows our every need and meets it with His love.

We each have burdens, cares, and needs;
and "Hungry hearts" our Father feeds.

For "Thirsty souls" He pours out drink...
To those who feel they're "Drowning," He will not let them "sink"!

To those who are lost; He shows the way.
He turns our Darkness into Day!

Our Father's love is "Tried and True."
He sacrificed His Son for you.

So, if you need a Valentine,...
God says, "I'm yours and you are Mine!"

If you are feeling alone or isolated today, remember how much God loves you! He is the truest friend and best "Valentine" I've ever had! And the Bible is worth a thousand Valentine cards to me! Share a smile with someone today. It could be the only one that they see... "Happy Valentine's Day!"

"Faith, Hope, and Love..."

by Marian Colton

Hope "Springs eternal," so does His love.
Both are gifts from our Father, sent from above.

Our Father sees our burdens and He lovingly shares
His strength and power to deal with all our "earthly cares."

Faith, Hope, and Love; we've been blessed with all three.
They are meant to share with the world, from within both you and me!

The Lord has a plan both for your life and mine,
To offer up Hope, and to let His Light shine!

So, my choice is clear; I'll share these with others:
Faith, Hope, and Love for my sisters and brothers!

You also have a choice as to what you will do...
"What actions will you take with what God has given you...?"

God has given us so many gifts as well as opportunities to use these gifts to bless others! We just need to open our eyes to see them and our hearts to receive them. Once we do that, our hands and feet can't help but to "go and share them with others!" We each are Blessed to Be a Blessing!

"March Winds..."

by Marian Colton

It's said that "March winds and April showers bring forth May flowers!"
But what about the "Winds of Change that cause our lives to rearrange"?

The death of a loved one, or a "loss of position," bring about a huge "transition"!
As winds and rains encourage new life; the "Winds of Change" seem
to stir up strife...

We aren't sure of where our lives are going; and our greatest fear is of
simply "Not knowing"...
BUT,
God is with us everywhere: He shares with us our every care.

So, when the Storms of Life begin to blow, straight to the Father is
where I go.
He holds my hand and "Walks me through." I know He will do the
same for you!

As the March winds blow and the "Storms of Life" rage on, I find that
walking close to the Lord keeps me grounded and feeling secure. He is
the Friend who sticks closer than a brother, and even the winds and the
waves obey Him! Matt. 8:27

**Special Note:

The PLC refers to the Brick Community Primary Learning Center: a school established in 1996–1997 to house the kindergarten population of the Brick Twsp. School District. It also houses the preschool disabled programs, the preschool autistic classrooms, self-contained and autistic kindergarten programs.

The Tribute was conceived and written during a very difficult week in February of 2008. On a Tuesday morning at 8 A.M., the interim superintendent of schools announced that at the Board of Education meeting to be held that very evening, a vote would be taken to close down our beloved PLC. It was a very dark day, indeed! We who had been a part of this special program since its inception eleven years before were stunned, discouraged, disenfranchised, and disillusioned! My poem put "a face" on our collective pain. The most touching moment for me was when I entered one particular classroom, the kindergarten teacher came to me with tears streaming down her cheeks and simply wrapped her arms around me and held me close... I knew that she felt as though someone understood her deepest intimate feelings with regard to our beloved school. My words gave a voice to her feelings.

UPDATE: In the spring of that same year, three new Board of Education members were elected, and the decision was made to keep the Primary Learning Center open. This truly was an answer to prayer!

A Tribute to the PLC

The PLC is the "place to be"
A model for how Kindergarten ought to be...
People come from faraway places,
To witness the joy on our children's faces!

It is a kind and comfortable place,
Where every student can discover "their place."
If some are special, it matters not.
Every student is "given a shot."

So much is learned, not just from books.
"Different kids" see no funny looks.
They mingle in with the school's population,
Who learn to accept them without frustration.

"Be nice" is the motto; and also "Be kind."
Encouragement and compassion are all that you'll find...
The teachers, the staff are trained in understanding;
Children can "try out their wings and trust for a 'safe landing.'"

From Principal Peg to Kathy and Rochelle,
The aim is for children to always do well.
We all work together; for that is the plan.
The PLC is a Community, the main goal of man.

My Daily Prayer

Be with me, Lord,
Throughout this day;
In all I do
and all I say.

Let my spirit
give you glory!
Let my lips, Lord,
tell your story.

Let me show
my love for you,
from the time I rise
'til night is through.

In the spring of 2010, the Brick Township School District made some drastic cuts to programs and personnel within the district. This had to be done in response to major cutbacks in state funding of public education in the state of New Jersey.

Here at the Brick Community Primary Learning Center, all special area teachers were reassigned to other schools. Reading programs were cut, the school social worker was reassigned, and even the vice principal position was eliminated!

It was a devastating time for our staff! Hearts were broken, and morale at an all time low.

This poem was my personal attempt to "put a face" on the emotions of the remaining staff members, to share our love, support, and encouragement with all of those who would be leaving (thirteen in all...). The poem was framed and presented to each one who faced reassignment.

Endings are often New Beginnings....

(A Fond Farewell...)

This program was special
due to each one of you.
May God's blessings continue
over all that you do.

Wherever you "settle"
to make your new "home,"
Remember, We love you
and you'll not be alone.

Our thoughts and our prayers
will be there with you,
to surround you with peace
and to comfort you, too!

Of this PLC Family
You'll always be a part.
We've worked as one body
and you share of our heart.

So now as you leave,
Moving on to new things
Take hold of the joys
"New Adventures" can bring!

May your future be bright
Filled with laughter and love.
May your life as a teacher
be blessed from above

M.C.

CPSIA information can be obtained
at www.ICGtesting.com
Printed in the USA
BVHW021818160122
626388BV00001B/1